Present Imperfect

Also by Ona Gritz

Welcome to the Resistance: Poetry as Protest
Editor with Taylor Carmen Savath
Galloway, New Jersey: Stockton University Press, 2021

More Challenges for the Delusional
Editor with Daniel Simpson; Prompts by Peter Murphy
Doha, Qatar: Diode Editions, 2018

Border Songs: A Conversation in Poems
with Daniel Simpson; Cover art by Juan Alberto Pérez
Georgetown, Kentucky: Finishing Line Press, 2017

On the Whole: A Story of Mothering and Disability
Bronx, New York: SheBooks, 2014

Geode
poems with cover art by Juan Alberto Pérez
Charlotte, North Carolina: Main Street Rag, 2014

*Tangerines and Tea, My Grandparents and Me: An Alphabet
    Book*
with illustrations by Yumi Heo
New York; London: Harry N. Abrams, 2005

Left Standing
New Women's Voices Series, No. 32
Georgetown, Kentucky: Finishing Line Press, 2004

Starfish Summer
with illustrations by Yong Chen
New York: HarperCollins, 1998

Present Imperfect

essays

for Carol,
   In friendship and
with deep admiration for
your beautiful work.

ONA GRITZ

Love,
Ona

POETS WEAR PRADA • Hoboken, New Jersey

Present Imperfect

Copyright © 2021 Ona Gritz

Poets Wear Prada
533 Bloomfield Street, Second Floor
Hoboken, New Jersey 07030
http://pwpbooks.blogspot.com

First North American Publication 2021
First Mass Market Paperback Edition 2021

Grateful acknowledgment is made to the following publications where some of these essays first appeared:

Bellingham Review; Brain, Child; Brevity; Catamaran Literary Reader; Hippocampus Magazine; JMWW; Lunch Ticket; The New York Times; Nine Mile Magazine; River Teeth; The Rumpus; Thread; Toasted Cheese; and Wordgathering.

ISBN-13: 978-1-946116-23-9   ISBN-10: 1-946116-23-8

Library of Congress Control Number: 2021945275

Printed in the U.S.A.

Front Cover Image: family archives

Author Photo: Wendy Setzer

In remembrance of
Angie Boggs, Raymond Boggs Jr.,
and Raymond Boggs III

Table of Contents

The Body Divided   3

Persuasion   8

Should I Feel Anything Yet?   12

Troll Pox   17

Present Imperfect   23

Here. Look.   31

Am I the Burning House?   34

Deluge   37

Speedometer Song   42

Streaming   44

The Spider Tattoo   47

She's Not There   50

It's Time   56

Love, Eventually   81

Acknowledgments   87

Notes   89

About the Author   91

Present Imperfect

THE BODY DIVIDED

D rops of rain slide down the dirty glass. From the back seat I ask why I feel less on the right side of my body. Though my father is driving, my mother doesn't turn toward me.

"Because your heart's on the left," she says. "Like everyone's."

MY CEREBRAL PALSY does that, works like Novocain, divides me in half. I can only test the temperature of water with my left hand. Eyes closed, I have to move a coin from my right palm to my left to tell it from a paper clip or a stone.

I don't know I walk differently. *Limp.* But then the new kid asks me how I hurt my foot. The gym teacher tells me to sit down. *That's a gallop, not a run.*

My two hands are sisters, Left beautiful in her grace. Right, *Clumsy-Girl*, with lesser jobs. Run the sponge down *Grace*'s arm after she's soaped and scrubbed the rest of the body. Hold Barbie still while *Grace* works the tiny buttons on her blouse, her small fingers steady and sure.

The damage is in the part of the brain that sends

messages to the muscles of the body. The messages are short-circuited, garbled, not unlike the messages I'm given about CP. *It's barely noticeable. Why do you walk like that? There's nothing you can't do. Here, let me do that for you.*

MY FRIENDS DANCE beneath twisted paper streamers. A boy takes the chair beside me, straddles it backwards, compliments my eyes. We sip watery Coke until the Bee Gees give over to Bread. David Gates is strumming the opening chords of "Make It with You," and I'm hoping the boy doesn't notice my limp as we head toward the dance floor. Think I see his smile flicker but not sure.

Laura Wingfield with her shyness, her small glass animals, her one bittersweet dance. Is this who I'm supposed to be?

IN COLLEGE, I discover that different is hip. This from girls in black turtlenecks, Indian print skirts, the habit of raising their voices at the end of each statement as though asking a question. I wonder, though only when stoned, why, if *different is hip*, we imitate each other with such care.

IN YOGA CLASS, where the mats smell of dust and feet, I learn the heart is barely left of center. It rests on the diaphragm so that as we breathe it moves like a buoy on a quiet bay. One of my classmates cries when she hears this, tears streaming artfully down her cheeks. I've cried in class too, hard sobs while doing the butterfly stretch. Feeling the pull in my inner thighs, I thought of men whose touches felt halfhearted in the dark.

I SIP TEA with a woman whose walk is like mine. We lean into the table, finish each other's sentences. *How did your parents explain it? Did you know anyone like us growing up? Dating. God, dating!* "Where have you been all my life?" I almost ask.

UNEXPECTEDLY, I CATCH my reflection walking, my gait a bit like a dance.

"BEAUTIFUL," HE SAYS, fingers grazing my uneven legs. I touch his rough chin, the perfect bones of his shoulders, the hollow of damp hair on his chest. This is how I know him in the dark: Left whispers the details. Right listens and believes.

Better half. Best to stay on my good side. You don't know the half of it.

RESTING AGAINST my right arm, the baby's head is a vague but pleasant weight. Only when I shift him to the other side can I feel the heat of it, distinguish the tapering at the neck. That leaves only my right fingers free to explore the skin of his face. I might be touching silk or rubber. His hair, too, has no specific texture, nor does it divide into single strands.

EVEN. WHOLE. Maybe it's not about the body and its limits. Maybe it's a destination, everyone hobbling there as best we can.

My son works his way toward me from the far end of the kitchen. New to walking, his steps are halting, a bit like my own. Flushed with effort, his face looks backlit. "Mama," he says, throwing his weight into my imperfect arms.

TEN POST-PREGNANCY pounds linger. I power walk the promenade, self-conscious about my awkward moves. But soon I'm adrift in the feel of my heart pounding, muscles working, how sunlight studs the slow-moving water at my side.

PERSUASION

What if I can't keep up?" I asked the social worker at the Y where I answered phones for the summer.

I was seventeen, leaving for college in just over a month. My list of worries also included whether my roommates and I would like one another, and if my clothes were right for the small artsy school I'd chosen that had, miraculously, chosen me too.

"Why wouldn't you?" he said. "You're smart enough."

He was in his late twenties or maybe early thirties but liked to sit on the edge of my desk as though he were a teenager as well.

"I'm kind of a procrastinator," I admitted, pulling Jane Austen's *Persuasion* from my backpack on the floor. "All freshmen need to read this before school starts, and I haven't even opened it."

Across the room, the sliding wall separating us from the gym stood partially open. Inside, a cache of boys played basketball, sneakers squeaking against the waxy floor.

He took the book from my hand and flipped to the back. "A hundred and ninety-two pages. And today's what?"

We glanced at the blotter that doubled as a calendar

and struck a deal. I'd read twenty pages every day, starting when I left work that evening, which meant I'd be done by the date he circled in ink.

"No missing a day, or I'll take you over my knee and spank you."

He said this, I assumed, the way the guys playing ball might say, "Miss this foul and you're a dead man." A joke lobbed at a friend to make a point.

Twenty pages a day. As it turned out, I liked Jane Austen. She was funny in a quiet, old-fashioned way. I stayed faithful until I didn't, skipping once to attend a party and again to watch a Monty Python movie on TV.

On the circled date, I worked the evening shift. I kidded with the ball players, took messages when the phone rang, gave newcomers directions to the bathroom. The social worker stayed in the inner office, appearing just once to ask about my progress in *Persuasion*.

"Almost done," I told him. "I'll finish it this weekend."

He drifted away until it was time to kick the basketball players out for the night. Next, he had to make sure all the lights were off in the upstairs classrooms. "Come with me," he said. A first.

Here is where I'm tempted to shift to third person, to make myself a character, to say *she* let him take her by the hand and lead her upstairs. *They* walked in companionable silence down empty halls, where he leaned into open doorways to switch off the buzzing florescent lights. But, of course, it was I who paused at each of those rooms and waited as, one by one, he darkened them.

He wouldn't really, I thought as we entered the last classroom in the corridor. But he dropped my hand, pulled out a desk chair, and settled into it.

"Come here," he said, patting his knee, and it was I who complied.

Afterward, we sat on the front steps, the glass doors of the Y locked behind us, the rough stone vivid beneath my stinging rear end.

"You understand why I did that, right?" he asked.

"To teach me discipline," I muttered to my feet in their scuffed sandals. "To help me in school."

"Exactly. Still, it's best we don't tell anyone. Not everyone would get it."

Here I'd like to say I lifted my face and stared at him until he glanced away, and that doing so released me from this story where a man might hurt me for my own good. But, in fact, I merely nodded.

"Deal?" the social worker asked, just as he had when he'd marked the date on the calendar.

"Deal," I told the unforgiving ground.

SHOULD I FEEL ANYTHING YET?

I t was the eighties, but we wanted it to be the sixties, those of us in divided Boulder who claimed Pearl Street, "the mall," as opposed to "the hill" where the CU students fratted or whatever they did besides look down on us through their Ray-Bans. They thought of us as out of touch hippies, which was fine since we thought of them as soulless. We, in the Jack Kerouac School of Disembodied Poetics, were writers. Better than that, we were poets. Of course, they couldn't understand our value and our depth. Few could.

That summer, I was nineteen. At the start of the year, on January 11th, my wild runaway older sister, who'd finally settled down with a sweet-natured bear of a guy, was killed along with him and their one-year-old son. But I didn't want to think about that, the latest and last of Angie's countless departures that broke my heart. I wanted to write stunning poems and make my friend David, a classical guitarist with green basset hound eyes, fall in love with me.

"He looks like Picasso's Blue Period guitarist," I told my good friend Kate, pleased with the artsy reference but also believing my words. David defined lanky. When he played Bach he leaned with his ear tilted toward the curved wood of his Yamaha as if it were whispering secrets.

"It's an old man in that painting," Kate pointed out. "It's called *The Old Guitarist*." She was worldlier than I, better read, a year older than my older sister who was now trapped at twenty-five. Kate thought of me, I knew, as boy crazy, which wasn't exactly true. It was more that the hope of being loved, like any hope, kept me from fading.

We had another friend named Dave that summer. Actually, there were several. But this particular Dave — bearded, burly — resembled my dead brother-in-law enough that my eyes slid away from his face whenever he stopped me on my window-shopping, jotting-in-my-notebook strolls down Pearl Street.

"You know it could be great for your poetry," he said one day, holding squares of blotter acid in his palm.

"Great for my poetry, how?"

With spit and breath Dave made the sound of an explosion. "It will expand your mind. Open you right up."

I, a girl who'd guiltily smoked pot twice in high school, stared at the tabs, considering. *No way my angel of a sister is gonna do that*, Angie would've said, mouth twisting into a wry smile. She who did it all. Heroin. Meth. But that was before. Before marriage, motherhood, being murdered. Now that she was the angel of the family, who should I be?

"How much?" I asked, pulling crumpled bills from my fringed shoulder bag. The acid looked like nothing, like lost bits of confetti. It would be good for my writing.

Days later, Kate and I sat by the creek in our wraparound Indian print skirts and swallowed the tabs with swigs of water from a suede-covered canteen. I thought of the button candy I ate in childhood, scraping the sugary dots off the paper backing with my teeth. This made me think of wax lips. Candy cigarettes. The real sixties. Angie — who was still Andra then — singing "Yummy, Yummy, Yummy" in my ear and calling me baby.

Kate was my one friend here who knew. Still, I felt an urge to say aloud, She's dead. They're dead. Even my nephew with his wet grin and chubby baby legs. Would hearing it make it finally seem true?

"Should I feel anything yet?" I asked instead, then saw my watch begin to spin.

A boy we knew from a class called Poetry in Daily Life — another Dave? — came across the footbridge. I waved, and my arm rippled like creek water.

"Hey kids," he said, licking a Dairy Queen cone. Rainbows flowed from his mouth.

"Amazing ice cream," I drawled, a record on too slow a speed. Kate's laugh echoed canyon-like around us.

I watched Maybe-Dave's word rainbows for a while, then he and Kate swapped heads. That's when I wanted my mind back, felt fear carbonating in my knees.

When you play, you pay, Angie used to say. She used to say a lot of things.

"Cut it out," I said now about the head-switching. It's what I'd shriek when my sister tickle-attacked. *I'm just playing, baby.* Again I gazed at my swirling watch, unable to read it, unable to make time move in either direction.

TROLL POX

When I was four years old, I caught a case of chickenpox that had been making the rounds in my neighborhood. My mother's reaction to those first telltale spots was to say, "Uh-oh!" but I felt delighted. My big sister had just gotten over the virus, and a few of my older friends. — kids already in school — had had it too. I was, of course, unfamiliar with the phrase *rite of passage*, but I recognized one when it spread across my skin as a connect-the-dots rash.

"I can't come out to play," I yelled from my window when my recently recovered upstairs neighbor happened by, pushing her doll carriage. "I've got chicken box now."

One morning, fifty years later, I checked my email and discovered I'd been contacted by a troll. He had read an essay of mine about marriage and disability that I'd had the good fortune of publishing in a national newspaper — a first for me. "I think your article got way more praise than it deserved," he wrote, "so I critiqued it here."

Staring at the link he'd provided, I felt only the slightest temptation to click on it. I'd gotten lovely responses to that essay from good friends, strangers, and even a few writers I

admired. Did I really need to know what this one
disgruntled reader thought? I moved his message to the
trash.

That was the end of it. Except it wasn't. I wondered
about this stranger who, for whatever reason, felt compelled
to tear me down. It was disturbing but also oddly flattering.
The next morning, I posted about it on the wall of an online
writers' support group. Even as I clicked the share button, I
recognized my four-year-old self, calling proudly out the
window about my chickenpox. I'd gotten trolled just like
writers in the big league do. I wanted people to know.

Members of the group quickly jumped to my defense, as
I knew they would.

Gross. Delete and move on!!!

How wonderful that your piece made him think?

Love your haters. They're your biggest fans.

Later, I tried to recall the first time I'd read an online
essay and noticed a rash of vitriol in the comments section.
Five years before? Ten? I remembered feeling shocked and
also queasy. What was it, I'd wondered, about this author's
writing that made people want to hurt her? The answer, I
now knew, was quite likely nothing in particular. Anonymity
together with access to a very public platform is a potent
combination. Hating had become a thing.

Since then, whenever I make the mistake of browsing
the comments section of nearly every online essay, I ask

myself is this really who we are. Are most people fuming, jealous, and condemning at their core? Inevitably, I had to ask an even tougher question. Am I?

The answer is no, but unfortunately, it is also yes.

I'm almost unfailingly kind to people. As a writer, I have no trouble genuinely celebrating the successes of my peers. Where I falter is in the private recesses of my brain. A city dweller, I've spent many hours of my life on public transportation, and that's usually where I hear it — the bitchy, judgy nattering that passes for idle thought.

Do you think we're in your living room? I silently ask the woman fighting with the person on the other end of her cell phone.

How many times can you use the word like *in one sentence?* I imagine saying to the teenager chatting with friends in the seat behind mine.

Perhaps worst of all, I catch myself thinking something along the lines of *are you really wearing those shoes with that outfit?* As though I'm some kind of fashionista, which, believe me, I'm not.

I don't know why I have such a vocal inner troll, though I suspect it points mostly to my own insecurities. Whatever the cause, once I began to notice, I worked to counter this tendency by consciously making positive observations as I passed through crowds in my travels.

Such soulful eyes. What an infectious laugh. And, yes,

Nice shoes!

Not unsurprisingly, I got waylaid on my road to recovery during the 2016 election season. Feeling confident Hillary would win, as did the pollsters and nearly everyone I knew, I took pleasure in watching her opponent prove himself to be a bumbling, lying, hate-filled, scandal-ridden, racist, ablest, xenophobic, sexist buffoon. (Truth be told, I've taken genuine pleasure in lining up those adjectives just now.) "We're so much better than this," I scoffed, even as I relished the taste of disgust like a SweeTART on my tongue.

Certain his presence on our airwaves and in our consciousness had an expiration date, I allowed myself this relapse. But during those long four years when that bombastic hater actually held the most venerated office in our nation, I came to see kindness as a crucial act of resistance. Meanness — like chickenpox, like COVID-19 — is a virus. Once airborne, it quickly spreads. And if the former president and troll-in-chief can be said to have any genius at all, it's that he knows just how to spread that particular germ. We either rage with him (hence the violence of the January 6th insurrection) or we rage at him.

But while rage may fuel us, it in no way nourishes us. Compassion does that, as does community, as does sharing our stories. This, of course, is where we writers come in.

These days we're lucky to have vaccines, which is to

say facsimiles of particular viruses can be put into our bodies to protect us against them. Not so with hate. But what we can do — particularly those of us whose work involves sharing experiences, ideas, and discoveries on the page — is make sure hate never has the last word.

PRESENT IMPERFECT

My son didn't seem to like me all that much in the first weeks of his life, and I couldn't say I blamed him. I may have managed not to drop him, or leave him on a grocery shelf as had happened in my dreams, but I nearly sat on him moments after laying him on my bed. And somehow I closed a snap on his little cotton sleeper with his skin pinched in between the halves.

I also cried constantly, but this was one thing we had in common.

"Everyone goes through that," my friends who were parents assured me. "Everyone finds it hard at first." But not all my graceless moments as a new mom were universal. Though my cerebral palsy is relatively mild, my dexterity is limited, and my balance — especially when my hands are full — can be less than steady. Still, it's subtle enough that it has often gone unnoticed. Even by me until the birth of my son.

For as long as I could remember, I'd wanted to be a mother and felt sure I'd be a natural at it. I worked as a children's librarian, and whenever a group of five- and six-year-olds came in for story time, they raced for the spots on either side of me so they could listen with their knees touching mine.

During my pregnancy, I read through piles of parenting books. I discovered there are two distinct camps. The Ferber faction believes that if babies are left to cry for allotted amounts of time, they learn to soothe themselves; while the Sears faction believes that if babies are attended to quickly and held much of the time, they grow up secure, having experienced the world as a loving, responsive place. Without having to think about it, I knew I would be a Sears mom and practice attachment parenting. *I'm here for you* was the first and most essential lesson I wished to teach my son.

I also pored over books on prenatal nutrition, some of which made me horribly anxious. When I read in a book on herbs that oregano could cause a miscarriage, I flew into a panic.

"We had Italian last night," I trailed my husband through our apartment to say. "We have it all the time."

"Plenty of pregnant women have eaten spaghetti without hurting their babies," he pointed out, adding wistfully, "You know, you used to be so easygoing."

He was right, I knew, but I couldn't help the fear that rose inside me like the steam heat that banged through our pipes. I was already so in love with our baby, it felt crucial that I do everything exactly right.

As for my cerebral palsy, I can think of two times it

crossed my mind while I was pregnant. Once when my midwife asked if I wanted to test for spina bifida or Down syndrome — I declined, insulted by the implication that a life with a disability may not be worth living — and again, in my cumbersome eighth month, when I joked to a friend that I was already used to moving awkwardly.

What didn't occur to me until after my son's birth was that motherhood required real agility. The first time I tried to nurse him, he couldn't reach my breast because of the sloppy cradle my uneven arms made for him.

After a harrowing day of trial and error, I was able to breastfeed, first with the help of nurses who propped pillows under my son, then later, on my own, by using a tire-shaped nursing pillow. Though that fundamental issue was solved, I soon discovered other problems. I wasn't able to bathe the baby without help, or swaddle him, or eat anything more challenging than a breadstick while nursing. And, as it was the only activity that kept my son from screaming like he was being dismembered, I nursed constantly. Hour after hour I sat in our glider rocker, and for all I was able to do for myself with a baby in my arms, I might as well have been in traction.

During his brief paternity leave, my husband did his best to help me. He brought me glasses of water with bendy straws to make drinking more manageable. He gave me his protein bars since I could eat them with one hand. But after a few days, he sighed loudly at each request. Clearly he felt my convalescence should be over. But my disability, of course, was permanent. It always had been, but since I'd rarely faced real physical demands in my childless life, it had never felt so prominent. In those not so long ago days, I thought of cerebral palsy as a cosmetic issue — I had a limp, which I hoped wasn't too noticeable. Now, glued to my seat, I felt humiliated and ashamed of all I couldn't do and of how ignorant I'd been about my own body.

"Sorry to ask again," I called out only when my thirst became unbearable. "But if you could just refill this glass . . ."

Visibly relieved, my husband returned to work after his allocated ten days. Before he left that first morning, he dug the camel pack he used for mountain biking out of the closet and filled it with water, then taped it to the back of the glider rocker, positioned so that I could take sips from the tube just by turning my head.

With that bag in place like a catheter, I sat in the empty apartment and nursed until I was dizzy with hunger. That's when I realized just how hard it would be to do something about it. I could carry my newborn into the kitchen if I did so with great care. I could probably even prop him on one shoulder long enough to open the refrigerator. But then what? With my one reliable hand cupping his head, I couldn't pour cereal or milk into a bowl. Nor could I use a spoon.

We had a bouncy seat for him, and I made a few attempts to place him in it, but he howled with rage before I'd even strapped him in. So, though feeding myself was impossible with a baby in my arms, in my arms he stayed, partly because of my almost religious belief in the tenets of attachment parenting, but mostly because I hated to upset my boy.

Now that we were on our own during the day, I quickly discovered other feats that were beyond me. Stairs had never been my forte, but as long as I had a banister, I did all right. But, in fact, my balance was precarious enough that, even if I held the baby in a carrier to free my hands, I couldn't be sure I wouldn't trip and fall. This meant we weren't able to climb aboard a bus, or visit our inaccessible town library, or leave our fourth-floor apartment those many times the elevator broke down.

Though these new limitations made my life considerably smaller, motherhood deepened it. Every day, I gazed into my son's wide blue eyes and fell more in love with him. Yet, the look he gave back was stern and, it seemed to me, judgmental. I imagined he saw me the way I'd begun to see myself, as klutzy and inept.

I rocked him and nursed, talked and sang to him. *Really?* his cool stare seemed to say. *This is the best you have to offer?*

Meanwhile, my husband worked long hours and often went out afterward with his coworkers to decompress. I had an open invitation to join them for drinks or late dinners, but of course, I was otherwise occupied. Caring for my son took all my time, and courting his affections took all my attention. He continued to respond to my devotion with an austere expression, which just made me all the more desperate to please him.

On Thanksgiving, when our boy was seven weeks old, we went on our first family outing, to visit my husband's aunt in the suburbs. As soon as we arrived, relatives whisked the baby from my arms and vied for turns to hold him. Though I was free to move about and gorge on the amazing array of appetizers that crowded all the surfaces in the room, I stayed on the couch like someone with Stockholm syndrome, eyes on my captor in case he needed me.

It wasn't until the end of the evening that my son let out his usual glass-breaking wail. My husband's aunt, who was holding him at the time, tried cooing and swaying, and rubbing his back. He just cried harder.

"I give up," she finally said and passed him to me.

I assumed he wanted to nurse, but the moment he felt me take him, he grew quiet.

"He knows who he wants," my aunt-in-law said, and I realized it was true. He missed familiar me.

As I felt my son settle contentedly in my arms that brisk autumn evening, I also felt a calm begin to spread inside me. I realized that, though I seemed more disabled now than before I became a mother, this didn't mean I actually was more disabled. Rather, I'd stretched myself and, in doing so, grazed the edges of my capabilities.

"You're teaching me who I am," I whispered into my son's tiny ear while around us our family all spoke at once, saying their goodbyes.

Not long after, my son smiled at me, and when he learned to reach out his arms, it was to reach for me. As things grew easier between us, I went easier on myself and worked to meet my own needs while taking care of his. I was still clumsy with him, but he didn't seem to mind. I came to see that my touch, no matter how inelegant, was home to him, just as my imperfect body had always been home to me.

HERE. LOOK.

My husband hadn't meant to render us in silhouette. He was a novice, the camera new and heavy in his hands. As we gazed out the window, he didn't realize that by aiming toward it, into the sun, he'd cast us in shadow, erasing specifics. I could be any woman holding an infant up to the view. I could be you.

Proud of this accidental art, he had a large print made and framed. When he hung it on our bedroom wall, I recognized its beauty, its quiet distillation of mother-love. But I also couldn't forget the flash of anger that still hummed in the air as the shutter clicked. "Him, him, him. It's always about him," he had yelled when I'd asked for a turn at the window where he'd been sitting, snapping shot after shot of a passing parade.

Him, that word, sputtered in triplicate, about our son still new and heavy in my arms.

And yet, eventually, I grew to love that black-and-white portrait. I could even say it told me what to do.

Here, look at how our heads rest on each other. Notice the negative space, its one border made by my chin and my child's ear, its other by my collar and the shoulder of his sleeper. That bit of light shaped by the way our dark forms touch — doesn't it resemble an open-winged bird? Doesn't it suggest flight?

AM I THE BURNING HOUSE?

I t's Family Day in my son's karate class, and he wants a turn at the front of the room to spar with me. We watch from the risers as other parent-child pairs perfectly mirror the moves Master Steve models, and the spouses and siblings around us snap photos and cheer.

I'm not even supposed to be here, but at the last minute, my ex (able, athletic) had to travel for business. So here I am, all the family my eight-year-old has on this particular Family Day.

"Please?" pleads this boy who never asks for much, so of course, I take his hand, let him lead me to the floor as he helpfully announces, "If my mom doesn't do too good, it's because she has cerebral palsy."

All eyes on us, I throw stiff and oddly shaped punches, answer his foot sweeps and knee strikes with shuffles. And though I tell myself no one gives a flying fuck if I can't do a roundhouse kick, I time travel to a school gym not unlike this one — *That's a skip, not a run. Bet you couldn't even catch a balloon.*

Later, on our way toward the door, Master Steve, in his white gi, motions me over. "You were really brave out there," he says. "That was a great thing you did."

Brave. The word echoes in my mind as my son runs ahead on the cold walk home. *Brave,* a word complicated by what I know Master Steve's day job to be: putting out fires, saving lives. I have a sense of how I'm supposed to feel about this. In fact, I go so far as to write a draft of this piece where I claim that stance. *Is the prospect of living in a body like mine scarier to him than entering a burning house? Am I the burning house?*

But even as I type those phrases, I'm thinking these ordinary acts of ours actually are a touch heroic. Our shame meters so often off kilter. Heat rising, as it likes to do, right to the surface of our skin.

DELUGE

During Sandy, my friend on the first floor saw a wall of water surging down Bloomfield Street. Another said it was like a brigade, that torrent of rain, like a torrent of boots marching in unison. Relentless, obscuring, the storm barged into basement apartments, turned couches into useless sponges, rugs into marshes, books into grounded birds.

In a story I often read to my son when he was young, a man is unhappy with how small and crowded his house is. He and his wife have many children, all loud and rambunctious. His bickering in-laws live with them, the bird in its cage constantly squawks, and the dogs are always at his heels. Desperate, the man goes to his rabbi for advice. "Do you have a cow?" asks the rabbi. Yes, the man has a cow. "Then bring it into the house," says the rabbi. The man, albeit incredulous, does as he's told.

One early spring day, a man from my poetry workshop lifted me up for a kiss in an otherwise empty elevator. I remember bending my legs at the knees as I went up so that I was kneeling on air. Did we spin? Everything was spinning in those first raw weeks of knowing each other. I felt dizzy and seasick. What happened once the elevator door opened to the bustling lobby? Who were we for the rest of that afternoon?

I experienced Sandy as sounds as I lay in bed in my fourth-floor apartment. As a whirling of wind, wind with a voice. An image came to me of my room floating on a sea, separated from the building that had always contained it, drifting off alone. When the power went out, I heard a popping sound as the lamp clicked off, followed by a vibrant silence. The ceasing of those household hums only noticed when they're gone.

The man with the cow tells the rabbi, voice trembling, "It's worse. The smell. The flies. The noise." The rabbi's advice? "Add your sheep. Throw in a few hens. Are there goats on the property? Bring them in too." Again, the man is dismayed but obedient. Soon, his home is a landlocked Noah's Ark, bulging at its sorry seams, the commotion deafening, the stench beyond words.

For weeks we kissed in noisy cafes, on park benches, in the fragrant pizza place inside Penn Station. We were heedless, but we weren't children. We weren't even young. We had jobs, bills. I had my boisterous boy to pick up from school. Only this flowering thing between us was homeless. "Get a room," a drunken man drawled as we caressed on the stairs to the Uptown 1. But a room with a bed at its center would attach certain words to what we had, words we weren't ready to claim.

Two days after the storm, a few shops with generators were able to open. The drugstore. Oddly, a florist. The corner newsstand. Still, it was eerie, empty. You couldn't cross certain streets because of live wires under the standing water. You couldn't walk far at all. On the side streets, I passed piles of sodden refuse higher than my shoulder. I talked to a young guy on a stoop whose car died under the weight of a felled oak. For a week I read by flashlight, opened cans of beans for dinner, lit the stove with a Hanukkah candle, turning our home into a kind of sacred space. My son — his cell phone and Xbox on hiatus — taught himself guitar.

The man goes to the rabbi one last time. "It's unbearable," he exclaims. The rabbi tells him to send all the animals back outside to meander beneath the trees. "Thank God," the man says, singing prayers as he rushes home to do this. That night, he gazes around the same crammed rooms that had sent him to the rabbi in the first place — his squabbling in-laws, pesky kids with their rowdy games, pets underfoot in the kitchen. Yet, on this last page of the book, the man sees his house as spacious. He sees it as palatial, which is how I expected to feel when, after seven sloweddown days of improvising, the lights came on and returned us to the easy sameness we had before.

Here is the part I don't like telling. While we were

kissing in public places, someone else loved me too. This was why we were such wanderers. That other man and I shared a home. We made certain promises, and I was breaking every one of them. Love can do that, even to someone who has otherwise always been loyal. That is, someone like me. Love can be the wall of water, the brigade of rain. It can drown the things you felt sure you couldn't live without, dependable things you thought were just humming along.

SPEEDOMETER SONG

My ex taught our son to do this. To angle the rearview and palm the key as he turns it. Which pedal makes the Jetta move when he presses his size 12 sneaker against it, and which slows and stills the car again.

His dad's exacting, our son tells me, and critical. My ex will yell, "Slow, I said slow!" so that our boy feels his heart leap against the tight sash of his restraint.

Now, though, it's just us: one long-legged guy in gym shorts and Red Hot Chili Peppers t-shirt; one mom, jacket tossed in the back seat, who never learned to drive. It's evening, and this stretch of wide suburban road is suddenly ours, not a single car visible for miles.

When he revs it, I feel it in my ears first, a kind of suction, then in my stomach, a slight thrill. I should scold him, I know, insist he stick to the speed limit. And I will, in a minute. But let me just take in the joy of it first. My boy, who is almost a man now, testing his power. Carrying both our lives, the way I once did, but with none of my fear.

STREAMING

It's the summer before my son leaves for college, the season, friends with older kids warn me, he's likely to rail, accuse, anything to cause a rift large enough to walk through to his new life. Mostly he's just quieter than usual, inwardly focused, except the times when, knowing I'm at my writing desk, he starts tossing a deflated soccer ball against the living room wall.

"Sorry, I forgot," he responds when I call to him to stop, a claim so outrageous I wonder if he does this less to rankle than to hear his own name spoken — loudly, firmly — to assure himself that we're still us, he's still here.

One evening, we watch *Friday Night Lights*: the pilot, the second episode, and though I've got a stack of dishes waiting, he's supposed to walk the dog, and I don't even care for football, we can't help but allow ourselves one more.

From then on, this is what we do, night after night, worry together about the star quarterback turned paraplegic; the bookish boy briefly loved by a troubled girl; the addict's son whose body is brilliant at sports. At dinner we talk about these Texans as though they were our neighbors, here in New Jersey. We gossip, predict, offer advice only the two of us can hear.

Too soon we finish the series, and for days, we're both doleful, aimless, grieving this loss in place of the one rarely mentioned, streaming toward us, and just weeks away.

THE SPIDER TATTOO

I 'm staring at the tattoo of a spider on the murderer's neck, at the crosshatched lines that form the top edge of a web, which disappears into the orange collar of his prison suit. I imagine it probably continues, spreading across his broad shoulders over that place where a pair of hands might have pushed him on a playground swing.

When I was little, my sister would take me to the park before supper, lift me onto the rubber seat, and let me fly. I loved that motion, the rhythmic squeak, the way she'd chatter behind me about the boys down the block. But then she'd make me go so high, I thought I'd catapult off that flimsy strap.

"Stop," I'd call, but she'd laugh and pull me back so that I'd soar even more, the swing tilting, and me holding on so tight the chains dug a web of red marks on my palms. Finally, I'd cry, and she'd slow me down and hug me, my wet face pressed into her smoky hair. Walking home, we'd hold hands, and that mix of joy and fear would move inside me until it changed into a secret between us.

Love does funny things, I think now and let myself wonder if maybe he loved her too, this man in the overheated courtroom, with the spider on his neck. The way love can push and pull, and push too far, it's possible, I suppose, that he loved her too.

SHE'S NOT THERE

"Your mother's your slave," a girl in the playground taunted.

"Is not!" I insisted, but even at six, I recognized the truth in her words.

My mom pulled socks onto my feet while I lay in bed to save me from the shock of cold tile, read to me in the bathroom when I had trouble going, brought sweaters out to whatever stoop I'd landed on instead of calling me home.

Meanwhile, my mom did none of this for my sister. She spat Andra's name. She screeched with anger. A curse or lie slipped from twelve-year-old Andra's lips, and she'd have to kneel in the kitchen, the cutout specks in the linoleum patterning her knees.

"Where's-my-sis-ter?" I chanted one afternoon, bouncing a pink ball in rhythm.

My mom kept browsing *The Pennysaver*. "Probably out with friends."

Andra didn't show up for supper, or after I finished my homework, or when I sat with my dad while he watched *Gunsmoke*. Outside, night had spilled all of its ink.

"She's always home by now. She should be here."

"You're right," my dad answered. "She should."

After that, Andra was gone often. Even when she pinky swore she wouldn't run away again. Even after we watched Dorothy hitch a tornado to technicolor Oz, only to pine for her black-and-white Kansas home.

At our home, Andra taught me to draw girls with slants of hair covering one eye. She explained why Fred Flintstone wore dresses and kept a pet dinosaur.

"Don't tell," she'd say, lighting a Kool in our hideout behind the garage.

Shaping her mouth into the O from my name, she sent bracelets of smoke skyward. I watched them spread and disappear.

The next time Andra returned from wherever runaways go, my parents threatened to send her away. "There are special schools for girls who keep looking for trouble."

It seemed upside down to me. Why banish someone whose worst offense was leaving?

Eventually, Andra was sent to what was described to me as a girls' boarding school in Upstate New York. I pictured a line of teenagers standing frozen in a row like Barbies at the toy store.

When we finally visited, we sat at a picnic table surrounded by trees and distant mountains. Andra probably told us something about her days there, but her words are as lost to me as the dialogue on the silent screen at the drive-in across from our motel. All I recall is needing to touch my sister, pushing her hair back from her pretty face.

A decade later, Andra visited me on my own grassy campus. I was eighteen, studying poetry and women's literature.

"Well, excuse me, Miss Educated," Andra quipped when I claimed to practically live at the library.

"Schoolwork," I mumbled, glancing away. I couldn't articulate that reading had long been how I escaped the painful imbalances at home.

Miss Educated. Listening back, through the years, I can hear pride beneath her teasing. But at the time, it felt like an indictment. Who was I to move so far past the sister I once worshiped? Her education ended in eighth grade, at the school I didn't yet know wasn't a school at all.

I also didn't know that when Andra arrived there, at thirteen, she'd already reached what for her would be late middle age. She died suddenly and violently the year after our stroll through my college campus.

It took thirty years — both parents gone, my own child a teenager — before I thought to call the library in Hudson, New York.

"My sister attended a boarding school in your town in 1970. Would you know what the name of it might've been?"

Hearing the word *reformatory*, my breath caught in my

throat. That pretty campus had been a lockup. I wondered what crime Andra could've possibly committed. Then I read about the Wayward Minor Act, which allowed the incarceration of children for deeds no more serious than skipping school or running away from an unlivable home. Under this state law, parents could bring charges against their kids simply for being difficult, simply for being kids.

The New York State Training School for Girls. The focus wasn't on education but on discipline and keeping the twelve- to sixteen-year-old inmates sealed off from the world. Inside, they faced forced labor, violence, sexual abuse, and long stretches in solitary.

Throw adolescents together, and they can be relentlessly cruel. Thankfully, they can also be loving and fiercely loyal. Training School girls fell in love, held wedding ceremonies, claimed other inmates as their children. The families they formed could be as rough as street gangs but also caring and protective in ways many of the girls, including Andra, never experienced at home.

"Don't tell," Andra often made me promise. I never did, but I also never asked.

Where were you, I'm asking now. What happened there? What got you through?

Without her here to answer, I turn to school records, case studies in yellowed books, memoirs by women who were once incarcerated girls — finally reading, not to escape but to bear witness.

"About time, Miss Educated," I hear my sister say.

IT'S TIME

It begins with an old song on the radio, one by the Monkees that you and your sister loved when you were small.

You think back to a time when the two of you were always singing. "If I Had a Hammer" on the front stoop before dinner. "The Cat Came Back" and "Boom Boom Ain't It Great to be Crazy" on car trips. "My Baby Loves Lovin'" as you walked beside her into town.

When you'd enter the corner store that smelled of newspapers and candy buttons, and she'd drape a long arm over your shoulder and pull you close.

"This is my baby sister," she'd announce to the boys who dropped their comics back on the rack and sauntered over. It made you feel protected, and at the same time, nearly famous.

Now you find yourself poring over her school records and staying up late, scanning photos onto the computer so you can zoom in on her wild-girl smile.

You even type her name into an internet search box, believing for just a moment that you might find a picture of your sister as a middle-aged woman on Facebook.

"You're such a goof," she used to say, twisting her mouth to hide her smile. She said it after you couldn't stop turning in your seat to get her attention as she sat in the back of your kindergarten classroom, teacher's helper for the day. She said it again as she patted at your eyes with wet cotton the time you tried on her false lashes and managed to glue both lids shut.

You're such a goof, you tell yourself now for even allowing the idea of finding her online flit through your mind.

For, of course, pecking out letters on a keyboard won't bring her closer, any more than pleading kept her from running away from home. From you. And of course, nothing you let yourself imagine will undo what ultimately happened to her, or her husband, or their eleven-month-old son.

What does come up is an article about Detective Hendrix, the man who used a phone bill and a breadcrumb trail of stolen goods to figure out that it was their apartment mates who killed them. Napoleon Hendrix, you learn, solved more than five hundred homicides over his long career; all while wearing his signature Armani suits, Stetson hat, and snakeskin boots.

Because the death penalty had been considered, but the jury decided on life without parole, on Google Books, in a law text, there is a chapter about the trial. And since your sister was nearly eight-months pregnant, the case is also cited elsewhere concerning fetal murder.

You reword your search to include your brother-in-law's name and find a blurb about the killings in an article listing interesting things to do in their city. The piece includes movie theaters, murals, dance clubs, and community gardens. You scroll through it, baffled until you reach the heading, "Places Where Bad Things Happened." The writing is jaunty:

> Sure, this is a great town with beautiful architecture and breathtaking views, wonderful people, first-class restaurants, sourdough bread, blah, blah, blah. But let's not gloss over the truth: this place is also a magnet for sickos.

Your sister's address is number five on a list of crime scenes. The paragraph about your family begins:

> Even many true-crime buffs don't know about the Crawl Space Killers. The year was 1982. The victims, an entire family.

"Ghouls," you mutter and afterward feel angry for days.

ACCORDING TO YOUR SISTER, two kinds of monsters hovered over your shared bedroom at night, and only she knew which were on duty. For the boy monsters, the mean ones, you protected yourselves by huddling together in one bed, whispering, and playing pretend. The girl monsters, she assured you, didn't mind if you went straight to sleep. She called them the nice ones, but you secretly preferred when the other ones were in charge and you had no choice but to stay up, a bit longer, inventing stories as she taught you to do while playing dolls. Though here in the dark, you didn't need to clutch Barbies in your hands to transform yourselves. "Let's say," she'd start, and you'd lean in, wondering what the magic in her mind would make of you.

ONE NIGHT YOU type in the names of the convicted killers and find a document that, once you get past the penal codes and attorneys' names, gives details you'd have learned had you or your parents attended the trial. You read that your sister's body — a towel still knotted around her neck — was found dressed in a nightie, panties, and one slipper. You are wearing a nightie, panties, and slippers as you read it. The words *safe* and *trusting* pop into your head. Your tea grows cold beside your computer. Your child sleeps down the hall behind a closed door. But it's the thought of your sister padding around her kitchen on a January morning that has your attention.

You see her warming a bottle of milk in a small pan of water at her stove. Her thick hair still an unbrushed tangle. The day still stretched before her like a promising road.

A nightie, panties, and one slipper. You remember

your sister in a pair of polka dot pajamas. They had a rip in the knee and were just a bit too short. *Only we get to see her like this*, you recall yourself thinking as the two of you sat curled on the couch watching *Bewitched*.

Out in the world, your sister was stylish. Hair frosted and ironed, skirts and tights in perfect combination. But here at home, with you, she could be plain. You studied the marbly skin on her shins, the beauty mark like a piece of dropped chocolate on her ankle. *Only we get to see her like this.*

FOR A BRIEF TIME, the two of you had matching summer pajamas, blue shorts with red-and-white striped tops. The following season you'd both outgrown them, and it was several years before you grew into hers. By then the two of you owned long prairie dresses. Whenever you saw your sister in hers, you'd run and put on yours.

"People will think we're trying to be twins," she'd complain. And if you begged her to pin your hair into a bun just like hers, she'd sigh and roll her eyes. Still, she did as you asked every time, sitting you in front of the mirror, working a comb gently through your knots.

NOW YOU FIND that the more you know about the murders, the more you need to know. When you come upon a document with the name of their landlord, the man who had found the first body, you write it down and call him.

The man, soft-spoken, kind, tells you how much he liked your sister's husband despite the couple's sometimes overdue rent.

"He was trying his best to take care of his family," the man continues, so when the other couple arrived to share expenses, he had looked away.

But then they stopped paying altogether; the landlord tried to reach them for weeks.

You press the phone to your ear as he describes how strange it was to enter their vacated apartment. To find one of the small bedrooms completely cleared out, the other filled with things, all in disarray. That very day he went to clean out the crawl space under the house and found your brother-in-law's body.

"It was the worst moment of my life," he says, confiding that he couldn't look at food, especially meat, for a very long time afterward.

⸻

SOON, YOU FIND yourself flying to the city where your sister and her family had lived and been killed. Gazing out the oval airplane window, you recall another visit to that city, decades before, with your parents.

You were a freshman in high school, your sister a street urchin at twenty. She had promised to meet you in the hotel lobby but never showed. All that week, you brought out her picture, flashed it to bus drivers, waiters, musicians on the street.

"Have you seen this girl? Have you seen her?"

Finally, your father said, "That's enough."

"We know she does this," your mother added, along with the cold, placating refrain of your childhood. "Don't worry. She always turns up. Like a bad penny."

AGAIN, YOU FIND yourself standing outside the apartment house your sister lived in with the one man who was able to hold her. "Marry me," he'd said the first time they met. Convinced he was handing her a line, she'd answered with a dare. "Get me a ring." And he did, the next day, from the five-and-dime.

The entrance to their building is blocked by a wrought iron gate. The facade is painted a sad, strange green. That it looks familiar has less to do with your visits as a teenager and more with how closely it resembles your sealed-up, ancient grief.

There, in an apartment at the very back, your sister had learned to cook, your nephew to crawl and later to pull himself up to standing. On the last day of his life, you happened to be there. You recall how he clasped your shoulder as he stood.

"Yay," you sang. And he grinned, a spot of drool glistening at the corner of his mouth. A new litter of kittens mewed inside a box on the floor. A rifle hung above the couch where a family portrait might have gone. Of course, you didn't yet know that rifle would be used to kill that baby's father the next evening.

⁕

IN ALMOST ALL photos of the two of you, you lean against your sister as if she is the thing that holds you up. In a favorite shot, at the beach, your sister, nine, crouches behind you, age three, her arms wrapped around your waist, her cheek touching yours. Both of you are smiling, she at the camera or at your father who is peering through it. Your eyes are nearly closed, your grin clearly a response to having her so near.

⁕

NOT FAR FROM the apartment building, you find the mortuary where their small funeral took place. Inside, a woman hands you some stapled sheets of paper, all that remains of the event. Tears stream down her cheeks as you talk with her about those long-ago murders. She hugs you, saying the hug is really from your sister, and you sink into it, wanting to believe those words.

What you don't mention is that you hadn't been at the service, thirty years before. Or that, until you sent for your sister's death certificate, just recently, you hadn't known there'd been any memorial at all.

Other families have funerals, and we have this.

AFTER THE SENTENCING, the only session of the trial you attended, you had written those words in your notebook.

Sitting on a hard bench, in the back of the courtroom, you had studied the couple who, hands cuffed behind their backs, awaited their fates. You had tried to see the thing inside them that would allow them to kill a pregnant woman, a sweet bear of a man, an infant. But they had appeared ordinary in their prison suits, which fit like medical scrubs or kids' pajamas. The woman had even worn a plastic baby barrette in her hair.

Now you wonder if your folks had known about the funeral and chosen not to tell you.

WHEN YOU WERE growing up, punishment for a runaway was reform school. Your sister was gone so much of the time, you lost track of whether she'd run off or been sent. She was home, gone, home again, a jump rope swinging skyward then slapping the pavement with no predictable rhythm.

AFTER THE MURDERS, the three of you lived without your sister just as you had before. As though it was the normal state of things. As though everything was fine. You remember your mother sighing and busying herself with a dust rag. Your father saying, "Poor kid was finally getting her life together" as he plunged into his toolbox and began rewiring a second-hand lamp.

You, of course, missed your sister. Terribly. But the feeling was simply familiar. And now, you're thinking that may be why it was the one emotion you allowed in.

Other families have funerals, and we have this.

Rather than mourn your nephew, you focused on the times you'd seen your sister ignore him, on the way your brother-in-law sometimes teased him, which to you seemed unkind. The little guy would have had a hard life, you told yourself, as would the one who died curled like a question mark inside your sister. These beliefs let you seal yourself off from your brother-in-law, let you forget his steadiness and his humor, allowed you to make him paper-thin like the photos that were all you now had of him.

Sometimes, in an attempt to break through your own numbness, you raged at your parents.

"Don't you care?" you'd shout, slamming the door to your room.

Alone, you'd take out the two rings that had belonged to your sister, a gift from a previous boyfriend who'd also hoped to marry her.

YOU RECALLED THE DAY your sister brought them out to show you, placing them in your palm. Slim, gold, with lines of inlaid pearl and a tiny hook and eye to connect them. A wedding set so delicate and perfect, you felt you should whisper in its presence. But then your mother snatched them from your hand and snapped them into her change purse.

"I'm holding these for safekeeping," she told your sister. "You'll just lose them or give them away."

The two of you sat, shocked into silence.

"She stole my rings!" your sister finally burst out, her voice shaking, incredulous.

Avoiding her eyes, you decided this was about safeguarding the rings, not alliances. You decided they were too nice to let disappear like everything else your sister touched. "She's just holding them for you," you said.

TWENTY YEARS LATER, on an autumn afternoon, you were running errands with your mother. Your son, an eight-pound bundle, was strapped to your chest.

"You should write a memoir," your mother suggested, as though you'd been discussing such things.

The idea struck you as laughable, especially given how small your world seemed in those first weeks as a mother, this stroll to the drugstore for diapers your one outing for the week.

"I think you've led an interesting life," she continued, citing your sister as an example.

Her name in your mother's voice seemed a foreign object. Something hidden away in a dusty corner, so long, its uses were lost to you.

"Yeah right," you drawled, sounding, you realized, exactly like your sister.

There was so much you could have asked your mother then. Did she have regrets? Did she grieve her? She'd made a space where you could finally bring up such things, but you stepped back from it. "These days I can barely write my name," you said.

⊷

ON THE TOP floor of the main library in your sister's city, a librarian hands you a fat binder of police reports where you find the unborn baby referred to as Jane Doe. "It was a girl," you say aloud, stunned by this brand-new knowledge, your throat closing in on the words.

You spend many hours in that library hunched before a microfilm reader, spinning from article to article so that the story unfolds much as it did through phone calls from the detectives when you were nineteen. "Body Found Rolled Up in Rug"; "Two More Bodies Found Under House in S.F."; "S.F. Police Have Not a Clue About Three Neatly Wrapped Bodies." This last one has a photograph of two tubular rolls of blankets lying in a junk-filled crawl space. It describes how the bodies were found amid poisoned rats and the domestic cats that died from eating the rodents. You had wondered what happened to the box of kittens, and now you know.

Finally you come upon the headline "Fine Sleuthing Solves S.F. Murders of 3." After that, the articles are about the killers rather than their victims.

"Florida Holds Couple Wanted in Slaughter of S.F. Family"; "Coroner's Evidence Could Link Couple to Family's Murder." This last one details how the coroner studied the flies, larvae, and maggots on the bodies to pinpoint the exact date of their deaths.

The couple who killed your family will be behind bars for the rest of their lives. This is the closest you can come to a happy ending. But your heart is stuck on those earlier articles, the ones where the victims are still unidentified. They could be anybody. This can be one of those news stories that leaves you feeling chilled and sad yet still able to go on with your day.

ONE EARLY EVENING you walk from the library to the law office of the prosecutor who tried the case. Together you sit at a dark wood table, going over what each of you knows.

There are the basics of the case, details you've read and that he confirms. Your sister was strangled and the baby smothered. The killers waited for your brother-in-law to come home from work, then shot him with his rifle. Together they hog-tied his body, wrapped it in bedding, then dragged it to the crawl space, where the bodies of his wife and son already lay. At least this is how you hope it happened for your sister's husband. Another theory is that they tied him up first and shot him execution style. That he lay there, helpless, the long barrel pressed to his head.

When it was over, the murderers drove through Nevada and then down to Florida in your brother-in-law's truck, selling his and your sister's belongings along the way. Among the goods was a ring your brother-in-law had bought your sister for Christmas, designed by a local jeweler, one of only two of a kind. The couple hocked it in Reno, using their own ID.

There are details only you know.

"I met the murderers," you say, and the attorney leans forward in his chair. "I was here, visiting."

THE MAN WAS tall, you recall, handsome. He had more tattoos than you'd ever seen on one person. His wife was a much older woman with a voice like she was holding back a cough. There, in that apartment, after you played with the baby and admired the kittens, you sat with this couple and watched an old movie on TV.

"Just look at that guy with the pencil-thin mustache," the man who would strangle your sister said as Errol Flynn swung from a mast in his tights and thigh-high boots. "Tell me that good-looking blond-haired man doesn't always get his way."

You were on winter break from college. A sophomore,

and sophomoric. Earlier that day, as you walked with your sister and her family in Golden Gate Park, you felt restless. You had made friends in that city: artists and writers with whom you planned to explore the art of the de Young, browse through books at City Lights, and recite your poems at open readings. *Miss Educated*, your sister had taken to calling you. "You're the body, I'm the brains," you had teased back, making her laugh. Right then, you felt you'd outgrown her.

Busy with friends the following day, you had put off phoning your sister though she'd asked you to call first thing. Later that evening, when your brother-in-law picked up, he sounded worried. He didn't know where your sister and the baby had gone. Over the next few days, you called repeatedly, but the phone just rang and rang.

When a friend suggested you contact the police, you shrugged it off, recounting the time your family flew in to see your sister and she never showed, and another when, after a week together, she left you sleeping in a hotel without a goodbye.

Your friend pointed out all that had happened before your sister was married. "Now she's got the baby, and she's *so* pregnant."

Still, you maintained, this was typical of your sister, and she probably was doing it this time because you had taken so long to call.

You and this friend drove to your sister and brother-in-law's apartment house. When no one came to the door, you wandered the neighborhood, poking your head into coffee shops, approaching people on park benches, anyone who might know them.

"I can't believe I'm doing this again," you said.

Finally, you flew home assuming, as did everyone — your sister's friends, your parents — that they had left because they couldn't pay their rent.

"She always turns up," your mother reminded you, "like a bad penny."

Then six weeks after watching Errol Flynn duel on your sister's small black-and-white television, you received the police call. Your brother-in-law's body had been discovered beneath the house, his state of decay placing his death at the time of your visit. Three weeks would pass during which you would run to the phone every time it rang, hoping to hear your sister's voice. Then she and the baby were found, all the more decomposed, only ten feet further back.

YOU ASK THE prosecutor about motive, a part of the story you could never fill in on your own. He tells you that the detectives came to believe it somehow started with your nephew. That his crying had angered the man, and things had escalated from there.

"But he was such a quiet baby," you say as if it

matters. The thought passes through your mind that he could have grown up to be quiet and unflappable like his father.

On a whim, weeks before this trip, you had Googled his name. A photo of a businessman came up on LinkedIn, someone who resembled your nephew enough, with his round cheeks and lopsided grin, that a shiver had passed through you. Days later, you would try duplicating the search, but the photo of the man would be gone.

"WHY NOW?" the attorney asks. "Why look into all this after so many years?"

You gaze up at this person who spent months and months of his younger life working to put your sister's killers behind bars. How do you admit to him that, though you are almost twice as old as your older sister ever got to be, you've spent much of those years allowing yourself to experience her death as just another of her many departures, no more or less heartbreaking than the rest? An answer formulates as you recall how you got here . . .

THE MONKEES CAME ON, when you turned on the radio, a song you've heard countless times. Only this particular evening, your parents long gone, it occurs to you that you might be the only person left who remembers how your sister had loved it. This leads you to reflect on how few people likely remembered her at all.

Not long before this, your son had threatened to run away. It was in the midst of an ordinary disagreement. He wanted a video game you deemed too violent. Your boy had just turned twelve, the age your sister was when she began leaving, and as he spat out his threat, you felt a jolt of panic. *What if he's a runaway like her?* you thought. *What if he's got the runaway gene?*

That night, after all was forgiven and you looked in on your sleeping son, you finally grasped that being a runaway wasn't a character flaw or a syndrome. That your sister's leaving may have been a sound reaction to her contentious relationship to your mom.

"She's impossible," your mother complained to your father, to other mothers, to you.

What adolescent isn't, the grown you thought, gently closing your son's bedroom door.

The realization pushed you toward some of your own dark corners — your brief and difficult marriage to your son's father, for one. You came to see how you intentionally chose someone more spoiled and demanding than you were as penance for having been the favored child.

You also began to better understand your appalling sleep habits. Though you'd always blamed your sister for the fear of abandonment that keeps you up late into the night, anxious and vigilant, you finally comprehended the other piece too. When you wake in the morning, every morning, already berating yourself for the smallest of mistakes, what you're feeling is guilt — over the times you betrayed your sister so as to protect your own safe place in the family, over getting to wake up at all. Survivor syndrome, you have learned, is an aspect of post-traumatic stress; numbness, a symptom too.

Uncried tears, you thought, the evening your son looked up from his science homework to tell you that the human body is 60 to 70% water. *At least for me,* you thought, *uncried tears.* For, of course, that last time you lost your sister, she didn't just leave. Her life was taken, brutally, as was her husband's and her son's, both of whom you also loved. As was the life of your almost-niece, who at thirty weeks was nearly fully formed and ready to be, like you, someone's little sister.

THE ATTORNEY SITS watching you with his kind, dark eyes.

Why now?

You think again of your son shouting at you that he'd run away. As he stood there that night — fists clenched, daring you — you finally realized that your big sister hadn't been the worldly, invincible person you'd believed her to be when she first snuck out the door. She'd been a child. A little girl calling for attention and for help. Of course, you couldn't have heard it then. You were a baby yourself. But thanks to your boy, who happened to inherit your sister's fieriness along with her teasing humor and sly smile, you hear it now.

"For a long time, I couldn't look directly at it," you tell the attorney. An abbreviation, imprecise, inadequate, but it's what you can manage aloud.

"I think I may have something," he says and, after searching his files, brings out a drawing by the man who, together with his wife, killed your family, an image of a skull with a snake slithering through its mouth and eyeholes, the word *Enforcer* calligraphed along the side.

In turn, you show him photographs of your beautiful sister and her strong young husband, of your little funny-faced nephew with his pudgy baby legs.

He looks at those photos for a long moment, then says thank you, so quietly you barely hear him.

BEFORE YOU LEAVE your sister's city, you pull out those photos again, prop them against a headstone that marks a single shared grave.

You sit cross-legged on the grass with your two nieces. They are the daughters of a much older half-sister raised apart and barely known to you until your teens. A relation who had taken in your runaway sister when she first went out West.

One of the nieces, who are both too young to have met their other aunt, asks if you own anything that once belonged to her.

"Two delicate gold rings," you tell them, admitting why you feel bad about having them.

"It's funny," your other niece says. "Our mom told us she loaned Aunt Angie her favorite jade ring and never got it back."

"There are a lot of rings in my sister's story," you say.

They already know about the ring that became a major piece of evidence when Phillip and Velma Henderson sold it en route to Florida, so you tell of the gum machine diamond your brother-in-law gave your sister the day after they met.

You also share something you recently learned from the trial transcripts you've begun to read. It seems your sister and brother-in-law hadn't actually been married.

"When she found out her mom and dad and sister were coming into town from New York," a close friend of theirs testified, "she bought an old silver wedding ring that I had."

It had stung you to come upon those words, to learn that your sister had lumped you with your parents, lying to all of you. Still, reading the testimony of her good friend felt almost like being next to your sister again, back in her confidence as in those days she blew smoke rings for you in the bathroom, relaxed in the knowledge that her secrets were safe with you.

You have a secret too. There's a ring she never knew about, one your ex-husband asked that you have tattooed on your finger to prove your love to him. Of course, you couldn't do it, couldn't ever get a tattoo, knowing Phillip Henderson had been — still is — covered in them.

The afternoon is passing, growing chill. Before you leave the cemetery, your nieces give you time alone at the grave.

TAKING A BREATH, you say, "Hey, Ray."

When you first met Raymond Boggs, you were a skinny, insecure teenager.

"Your picture doesn't do you justice," he'd said, the exact words you had needed to hear.

"Thank you for being so loving to my sister," you tell him now.

Then you talk to your nephew, also named Ray, whom you held within moments of his birth. He had six toes on one of his little feet, another fact, you realize, you're probably the only person left in the world to know.

"You were such a good baby," you whisper. "I'm sure you would have been an amazing man."

Next you talk to Jane Doe Boggs, your niece who never made it to birth.

"I wish you had seen the sky," you tell her. "I wish you got to press your face into your mother's thick hair."

Finally you speak to Angie, your first love in this life.

"You taught me about being happy," you tell her. "You were the brightest light in our house."

HERE IS WHERE I finally cry. Because, of course, this isn't your story but mine, and it's time for me to claim it.

Andrea Susan Gritz, who we had called Andra, took the name Angie from a Rolling Stones song and the name Boggs when she unofficially married a kind, adoring man. She named her son Ray like his father, like a bar of sunlight. She hoped her second born would be a girl. If they had a name for her in mind, I never knew.

Angie liked the smell of gas stations. Her favorite snack had once been celery with cream cheese. "Touch tongues," she used to say when we were little, and I'd tap my tongue to hers for a second. An intimate flicker. A secret sister moment.

Now, under a moody Northern California sky, I start to recite the Mourner's Kaddish but change my mind and sing "I'm a Believer" instead. When we were small, Angie and I danced on our beds whenever the Monkees came on the radio.

"Try this," she'd say, wriggling her hips for the twist, or corkscrewing her body downward, nose held, for the swim. We'd do this with our pajama bottoms on our heads, pretending to be beautiful young women with long flowing hair.

Through most of our growing up, we saw so little of each other, we took to trading things when we were together. One 45 for another, a pair of jeans for a flouncy skirt. Now, I peel a ring off my finger and bury it in the dirt. Such a small thing, a little circle of silver framing a hole. But small things were all I'd ever been able to give my sister. I could keep her smoking a secret. Trade my leather jacket for her frayed sweater, knowing she's gotten the better deal. Be the one person she could count on to always be thrilled to see her.

Except for that last time when, not knowing it would be the last time, I felt restless and superior. For so long, I couldn't let myself grieve or even miss her because it meant recalling those feelings.

I SIT AT the grave awhile longer, freshly cut grass tickling my ankles, sun bright despite the clouds. These days I miss her something awful. Only *awful* maybe isn't the right word as my missing Angie has brought her back a little.

I pat at the soil above the buried ring. "Sorry I took so long," I say.

LOVE, EVENTUALLY

O ne night when I was very young, I lay in my bed across from my older sister's and described what I planned to look like when I grew up. My wavy brown hair would be straight and blonde. My eyes, now the color of over-steeped tea, would turn blue. I wore a leg brace to bed in those days, a metal rod that buckled with a leather strap below my knee and attached to an ankle-high shoe. Though I felt the weight of this contraption as I spoke, and I knew I limped because the meanest girl on our block had told me, it went without saying that the beautiful future me would walk, even run, with grace.

My sister listened without comment. She'd taught me to put pajama bottoms on my head, so when we danced like go-go girls, it felt like we had long, swingy hair; and to dress our Barbies, with their shapely symmetrical legs, in fashionable outfits for their dates with G.I. Joe and Ken. The truest world I knew was the one my sister and I dreamt up. It made perfect sense to me that who we got to be in the mystical world of adulthood was completely up to us.

I have a form of cerebral palsy known as right hemiplegia, which essentially means only half my body is

affected. My right limbs are tight, the muscles
underdeveloped, and the fingers of that hand lack the
dexterity and fine motor skills of those on my left.

Years ago, a friend who worked as a dance therapist
told me of her experience with hemiplegic children. She
suggested that while left hemiplegics respond well to
straightforward instruction ("Raise your arm as best you
can"), right hemiplegics do better with more poetic
description ("Imagine you're reaching for the stars"). This
may be due to differences in the left and right brain. Left
hemiplegics have undamaged left hemispheres and tend to
be pragmatic. Meanwhile, my compatriots and I depend on
our undamaged dreamy and artistic right hemispheres.

In my teens and twenties, if I considered my CP at all, it
was through the lens of vanity. How noticeable was my
limp? Was I pretty despite it? The answer, I assumed, was
in the response I got from men. This was hard to decode.
Apparently, I was appealing enough to sleep with but not to
be picked as a girlfriend.

Then I met a young man. He was handsome, athletic,
and crazy about me. We moved in together, got engaged,
and my old habit of magical thinking surfaced. I believed his
love canceled out my disability. Unfortunately, we had little
in common. He liked the thrum and excitement of clubs. I
preferred small gatherings and intimate conversation. He
was happiest on a mountain bike; I was happiest at home

with a book. Because of our disparate interests, we maintained largely separate social lives. I didn't actually mind this. My free time was given over to girlfriends, just like when I was single. Only now I had the perk of coming home to a handsome, affectionate man.

One of my closest friends was, and remains, a woman I came to know shortly before I was married. Hope was my first friend with cerebral palsy. Our connection was immediate and intense, fueled as it was by a sense of recognition that my imminent marriage lacked. I had other friends who got me in a visceral, finish-each-other's-sentences kind of way. But only Hope could finish the sentences I'd never before said aloud, the ones about how it felt to live in a non-normative body. Before we met, neither of us knew we craved those conversations, but we were starved for them. Though we shared many interests, it would be weeks before we could tear ourselves away from the topic of disability long enough to discover what they were.

Without realizing it, I began to live a kind of split existence. By loving Hope I was learning to love a part of myself I'd deliberately ignored. Still, I continued to rely on the myth that being married to an able-bodied man meant I wasn't truly disabled. Only now do I see that he gave me a safe perch from which to peek at my identity as a disabled woman. I could take it on briefly, explore how it felt to claim it, and then go home to my real life. That is my life of pretend.

Reality finally hit when we had a child. My husband eventually developed a very loving relationship with our son, but he wasn't exactly hands-on in the beginning. Meanwhile, I hadn't understood that caring for an infant is physically challenging work. Some tasks I could manage by making adaptions, but for many, I needed to ask for help.

At first, I felt deeply embarrassed by what I perceived as my ineptitude. But at some point, while I was busy figuring out ways to get everything done, I forgot about the shame.

By the time Ethan turned three, the physical demands of mothering had lessened, and I could focus on the parts that came easily — talking with him, reading together, entering into his imaginary worlds. A year later, my husband and I divorced. Thankfully, by then I understood that my tie to him wasn't what made me whole.

In a long-ago interview with Bill Moyers, the poet Maya Angelou revealed her theory that most women marry other people's husbands. She didn't elaborate, but I immediately understood. Out of hopefulness, impatience, insecurity, or for a thousand other reasons, we, too often, rush into relationships that are poor fits for us, robbing our partners and ourselves of other more promising connections. It struck me as likely that those of us with disabilities are especially susceptible to this.

"I have finally married my own husband," Angelou went on to say.

Many years after my first marriage, so did I.

Dan and I met in a poetry workshop.

"Of course," Hope said, when I told her that my new love was not only a fellow writer but someone with a disability. "It's like you guys are the same person, only one's male and one's female," said Ethan — not entirely as a compliment — who was eight at the time.

It's true that Dan and I are very similar. We're both romantics yet also fiercely independent. We're introspective to the point of obsession. Though he's a decade older, we share a love for the music of his teen years. And long before we met, many of the same novels and poetry books lined our shelves.

As for our disabilities, they're nothing alike. Dan was born blind, and that library of his is largely in braille and audio. He sees light but no shapes or objects.

"Does the light have a color?" I asked when first getting to know him. But, of course, since light is all he can see, he has no way to know.

Dan confided to me that, back in high school and college, he knew how to use a cane but chose to walk without one in an attempt to blend in. Back then, he also sought able, sighted women rumored to be beautiful. When I shared my stories in kind, I was struck, just as I'd once

been with Hope, by how little had to be explained.
Clearly,though our disabilities are different, the emotions
and their residue are much the same.

These days, disability is a mere factor in our daily
routines. It's there when I need to proofread Dan's Word
docs for formatting inconsistencies, or tell him which bottle
contains Tylenol and which the dog's allergy meds, just as it
is when he has to climb ladders to change our smoke alarm
batteries, or hold me upright as we walk on ice-slick streets.
I read the mail to Dan, of course, but also poems and
stories. He reads to me too, running his fingers along pages
of braille as though skimming them through water. And yes,
his touch on my skin is just as attentive and skilled.

Disability has also earned a central place in our
creative work. We've both written extensively about living in
these unique bodies of ours and spoken at universities and
on panels about disability poetics. Many of our friends are
artists and writers with disabilities. It's a rich life, one I
never could've imagined despite my famously active
imagination.

Still, had the possibility of this loving bi-disability
marriage presented itself to us years earlier, I don't think
either of us would have been ready. We needed the right
combination of fallacies, wrong turns, and formative
relationships to lead each of us exactly here.

Acknowledgments

My thanks to the editors of the various publications where these essays originally appeared, sometimes in a slightly different format or version:

Bellingham Review	"The Body Divided" (as "On the Whole")
Brain, Child: The Magazine for Working Mothers	:"Present Imperfect"
Brevity's Nonfiction Blog	"Troll Pox"
Catamaran Literary Reader	"Speedometer Song"
Hippocampus Magazine	"Persuasion"
JMWW Journal	"Deluge"
Lunch Ticket	"She's Not There"
The New York Times	"Love, Eventually"
Nine Mile Magazine	"The Spider Tattoo"
River Teeth	"Here. Look."
The Rumpus	"It's Time"
Thread	"Should I Feel Anything Yet?"
Toasted Cheese Literary Journal	"Streaming"
Wordgathering	"Am I the Burning House?"

"Love, Eventually" was reprinted in the anthology *About*

Us: Essays from the Disability Series of The New York Times, edited by Peter Catapano and Rosemarie Garland-Thomson, 2019.

"It's Time" was listed as Notable in *The Best American Essays*, 2016.

"The Body Divided" placed second for the *Bellingham Review*'s 2008 Annie Dillard Award for Creative Nonfiction and was reprinted in the 25th Anniversary Issue of *The Utne Reader*.

Notes

"She's Not There":

1. Kenneth Wooden, *Weeping in the Playtime of Others: America's Incarcerated Children* (McGraw-Hill, 1976).

2. Nina Bernstein, "Punishing Women, Punishing Girls," Fellowship Stories, Alicia Patterson Foundation, aliciapatterson.org, 1996. https://aliciapatterson.org/stories/punishing-women-punishing-girls

3. Nina Bernstein, *The Lost Children of Wilder: the Epic Struggle to Change Foster Care* (Vintage Books, 2002).

4. Lillian Ambrosino, *Runaways* (Beacon Press, 1971).

5. Rose Giallombardo, *The Social World of Imprisoned Girls: A Comparative Study of Institutions for Juvenile Delinquents* (John Wiley & Sons, 1974).

6. Susanna Kaysen, *Girl Interrupted* (Vintage, 1994).

7. Jan Kerouac, *Baby Driver* (Thunder's Mouth Press, 1998).

"It's Time":

1. Jim Herron Zamora, "S.F.'s Top Sleuth Calls It Quits After 34 Years," *San Francisco Gate*, September 12, 1999.

2. Welsh S. White, *Litigating in the Shadow of Death: Defense Attorneys in Capital Cases* (University of Michigan, 2006).

3. "Places Where Bad Things Happened," *San Francisco Bay Guardian*, April 23, 2003.

4. People v. Henderson, 225 Cal. App. 3d 1129 (1990).

5. "Body Found Rolled Up in Rug," *San Francisco Chronicle*, March 1, 1982.

6. "Two More Bodies Found Under House in S.F.," *San Francisco Chronicle*, March 20, 1982.

7. Larry Maaz, "S.F. Police Have Not a Clue About Three Neatly Wrapped Bodies," *San Francisco Examiner*, March 20, 1982.

8. "Fine Sleuthing Solves S.F. Murders of 3," *San Francisco Examiner*, April 30, 1982.

9. Jennifer Foote, "Florida Holds Couple Wanted in Slaughter of S.F. Family," *San Francisco Examiner*, April 30, 1982.

10. Dennis J. Opatrny, "Coroner's Evidence Could Link Couple to Family's Murder," *San Francisco Examiner*, December 1, 1982.

11. *Diagnostic and Statistical Manual of Mental Disorders*, 5th edition (American Psychiatric Publishing, 2013).

"Love, Eventually":

1. Charles Grinker and Mert Koplin, "A Portrait of Maya Angelou," *Creativity with Bill Moyers*, season 1, episode 1, PBS WNET, October 1, 1982.

About the Author

Ona Gritz is the author of the poetry collection *Geode*, a finalist for the Main Street Rag Poetry Book Award, and *On the Whole: a Story of Mothering and Disability*, a memoir that Paige Bennett of BlogHer says, "reads like poetry" and "should be required reading for all new moms." Together with her husband, Daniel Simpson, Ona co-wrote *Border Songs: A Conversation in Poems* and co-edited *More Challenges for the Delusional*, an anthology of prompts, prose, and poetry. A long-time columnist for *Literary Mama*, her work has appeared in *The New York Times, The Guardian, The Utne Reader, Ploughshares, The Bellevue Literary Review, Beauty Is a Verb: The New Poetry of Disability*, and many other journals and anthologies. Ona's children's book, *Tangerines and Tea, My Grandparents and Me*, was named Best Alphabet Book of 2005 by *Nick Jr. Family Magazine*, and one of six Best Books of the year by *Scholastic Parent & Child Magazine*. Among her recent honors are two Notable mentions in *The Best American Essays*, a Best Life Story in *Salon*, and a winning entry in The Poetry Archive Now! WordView 2020 Collection. Ona lives with her family in Lansdowne, Pennsylvania.

ABOUT THE TYPE

Text for this book is set in Bookman Old Style, designed by Ong Chong Wah (b. 1955) for Monotype and released in 1990. The Malaysian-born graphic and font designer studied and worked in England, mostly in advertising prior to Monotype. His credits also include the ever-popular Footlight (Monotype) and Ocean Sans (Adobe) among a total of nine type families.

Ong's Bookman Old Style is characterized by the near-vertical stress of its face, heavy type color, wide letters, and the somewhat taller lowercase characteristic of hymn and classic children's books. Ong based his digitized design on various 1960s and 1970s phototypesetting revivals of Alexander Phemister's classic Old Style Antique (circa 1858) cut for the Miller and Richard foundry in Edinburgh, Scotland, as a "modern" recasting of the Caslon typeface cut by William Caslon in the 1720s.

Despite the "Old Style" tag and look — or perhaps because of it — Ong's design continues to prevail. Title designer Victoria Vaus selected Bookman Old Style for the main title of the 1999 film *Election*, a high school comedy starring Matthew Broderick and Reese Witherspoon, directed by Alexander Payne. Later the typeface was adopted for the original Tumblr logo (2007–2013) by designer Peter Vidani — prior to Yahoo! acquisition mid-2013. Bookman Old Style was chosen here for its legibility, classic storybook styling, and general good humor.

Made in the USA
Middletown, DE
28 November 2021